This book belongs to

Copyright © 2024 Kate Pricklewood
All rights reserved.
ISBN: 978-1-0685583-1-3

A Prickly Christmas Adventure

Kate Pricklewood

It was Christmas Eve in the Hedgehog family's cozy little burrow, and excitement buzzed in the air like snowflakes dancing in the breeze. Holly, Henry, and Hazel could hardly contain their energy. They had been waiting all year for this special night when Father Christmas would zoom through the sky in his sleigh, bringing gifts for all the forest animals.

Mommy Hedgehog was in the kitchen, humming to herself as she baked her famous cinnamon nut bread. The smell filled the burrow, making Daddy Hedgehog's tummy rumble. He peeked into the kitchen and rubbed his belly. "Do you think Father Christmas might leave me an extra slice of your nut bread in my stocking?" he asked with a mischievous grin. Mommy Hedgehog chuckled. "Only if you promise not to eat the whole loaf before he arrives!"

Meanwhile, Holly, Henry, and Hazel were bouncing around the living room, decorating a tiny tree they'd found just outside their burrow. It was covered in shiny berries, pinecones, and strands of frosty grass they had gathered from the forest.

"Look, I made a star!" Henry called proudly, as he placed a slightly wonky pinecone at the top of the tree.
"It's a little crooked," Holly giggled.
"That's okay," Hazel said, "Father Christmas won't mind as long as we leave him some snacks!"

"Snacks!" Henry suddenly looked serious. "What if he's super hungry this year? What if he brings an extra reindeer, and they all need snacks?"

Daddy Hedgehog popped his head into the room. "Don't worry, Henry! We'll leave him some of Mommy's nut bread and berries."

As night fell and the stars twinkled in the sky, the Hedgehog family gathered around the Christmas tree. They laid out a small plate of nut bread, a handful of berries, and — just in case — some of Mommy Hedgehog's special honey-glazed acorns.
"Do you think we'll hear the sleigh bells?" Hazel asked, her eyes wide with wonder.
Mommy Hedgehog smiled "If we listen very closely, we just might!"

Soon it was bedtime. Mommy and Daddy tucked the little hedgehogs into bed, and after much giggling, wriggling, and whispering, they finally drifted off to sleep, dreaming of snowy hills and twinkling lights.

But later that night, something magical happened. A soft "whoosh" of wind woke Holly from her sleep. She blinked and sat up, peeking out the window. There, shimmering in the moonlight, she saw a sleigh gliding through the forest, pulled by majestic reindeer!

Unable to contain her excitement, Holly nudged her siblings awake. "Wake up! Wake up! Father Christmas is here!" she whispered loudly.

Together, they tiptoed to the living room and peeked out the window. Sure enough, Father Christmas had landed his sleigh right outside their burrow! His reindeer munched happily on some of the berries they had left out.

But then something unexpected happened. As Father Christmas reached into his sleigh for their presents, one of the reindeer — Rudolph, with his shiny red nose — sneezed! "Achoo!" Rudolph let out a mighty sneeze, and the gifts went flying into the snowbank!

Father Christmas burst out laughing, giving Rudolph a playful nudge. "Well, that's one way to deliver presents! A little snow never hurt anyone, right?"
Rudolph sniffled and gave an innocent shrug. "Oops! At least it wasn't reindeer flu!"
Holly, Henry, and Hazel giggled from inside the burrow.

Daddy and Mommy Hedgehog, who had also woken up from all the excitement, stepped outside to help. "Need a hand, Father Christmas?" Daddy asked, trying to keep a straight face. Father Christmas laughed, his belly jiggling like a bowl of jelly. "Oh, thank you, Mr. Hedgehog! These snowy nights can get a little tricky sometimes."

With the Hedgehog family's cheerful assistance, Father Christmas carefully collected the gifts scattered on the snowy ground, each one wrapped in colorful paper and adorned with shimmering bows.

He placed them with great care beneath the twinkling branches of the family's Christmas tree. As he finished arranging the last present, he turned to the wide-eyed children and gave them a warm, knowing wink. "You've been wonderfully good this year!" he said with a twinkle in his eye. "Enjoy every bit of your presents, my little hedgehogs."

Before he left, Father Christmas took a big bite of the nut bread and smiled. "Delicious! Just what I needed to finish my night!"

But as Father Christmas climbed back into his sleigh, Holly noticed something sparkling on the ground. "Wait! You forgot something!" she called out, rushing over and holding up a shiny silver bell that had fallen from Rudolph's harness.

Father Christmas smiled and waved. "Keep it, my dear. It's a little Christmas magic for you to remember this night!" With that, he flew off into the sky, the jingling bells growing fainter and fainter until they were just a memory.

The next morning, the Hedgehog family gathered around their tree, laughing and sharing stories of the magical night. Holly held the silver bell close, knowing that they had all been part of something special.

Holly gasped with delight as she opened a box to find a magnificent crown made of forest flowers — just like the one she'd always dreamed of.

Henry grinned when he unwrapped a miniature explorer's kit, complete with a magnifying glass, a little compass, and a small journal for writing down all his discoveries. "Now I can track every single butterfly!" he exclaimed.

Hazel squealed with joy as she found a beautiful music box. When she opened it, a small hedgehog spun in circles to a sweet, tinkling tune.

Mommy Hedgehog smiled as she received a soft, woolen scarf in her favourite shade of green, perfect for keeping her cozy during the chilly winter months.

Daddy Hedgehog laughed when he unwrapped his present — a brand new pair of sturdy hiking boots. "Just what I needed for our next adventure! Maybe now I'll stop tripping over my own paws!"

"Well," Daddy Hedgehog said, munching on a leftover piece of nut bread, "if every Christmas is this exciting, we might need a bigger burrow to fit in all the fun!"
And with that, the Hedgehog family celebrated Christmas together, full of laughter, love, and the warmth of being together — just as it should be.

Daddy Hedgehog

Playful and a bit mischievous, Daddy Hedgehog is always ready with a joke or a funny remark. He has a big appetite for both Mommy's cooking and life's little adventures, making sure the family is always laughing together.

Mommy Hedgehog

Caring and nurturing, Mommy Hedgehog is the heart of the burrow, filling it with warmth, delicious nut bread, and love. She effortlessly brings joy to the family with her baking and gentle sense of humor.

Father Christmas

Jolly and full of magic, Father Christmas brings joy and laughter to the Hedgehog family. Even when things don't go quite as planned — like when Rudolph sneezes — his cheerful spirit never fades.

Holly

Holly is the oldest of the Hedgehog siblings, full of curiosity and wonder. She's always the first to notice something magical, like Father Christmas's sleigh, and loves to keep her siblings excited and in awe of the world around them.

Henry

Henry is adventurous and imaginative, always thinking of grand ideas like how Father Christmas might need extra snacks for his reindeer. He's a little clumsy but has a big heart and a love for exploring the forest.

Hazel

The youngest of the Hedgehog trio, Hazel is sweet and thoughtful, often bringing the group together with her kind spirit. She loves music, and her innocence adds a gentle charm to the family's holiday adventure.

www.ingramcontent.com/pod-product-compliance
Lightning Source LLC
LaVergne TN
LVHW071653060526
838200LV00029B/445